D0916370

The Honey of Earth

Also by David Graham

Second Wind
Magic Shows

Local News: Poetry About Small Towns
(poetry anthology, co-edited with Tom Montag)
After Confession: Poetry as Autobiography
(essay anthology, co-edited with Kate Sontag)

Stutter Monk (chapbook)
Greatest Hits 1975-2000 (chapbook)
Doggedness (chapbook)
Common Waters (chapbook)

The Honey of Earth

David Graham

Terrapin Books

Terrapin Books
4 Midvale Avenue
West Caldwell, NJ 07006

www.terrapinbooks.com

ISBN: 978-1-947896-19-2
LCCN: 2019940778

First Edition

Cover art: *Piseco Kitchen*, oil on board
by Lee Shippey

Above all

for Lee

again and again

Contents

IV

The honey of heaven may or may not come,
But that of earth both comes and goes at once.

—Wallace Stevens

|

The Dogs in Dutch Paintings

How shall I not adore them, snoozing
right through the Annunciation? They inhabit
the outskirts of every importance, sprawl
dead center in each oblivious household.

They're digging at fleas or snapping at scraps,
dozing with noble abandon while a boy
bells their tails. Often they present their rumps
in the foreground of some martyrdom.

What Christ could lean so unconcernedly
against a table leg, the feast above continuing?
Could the Virgin in her joy match this grace
as a hound sagely ponders an upturned turtle?

No scholar at his huge book will capture
my eye so well as the skinny haunches,
the frazzled tails and serene optimism
of the least of these mutts, curled

in the corners of the world's dazzlement.

Listening for Your Name

As a father steals into his child's half-lit bedroom
slowly, quietly, standing long and long
counting the breaths before finally slipping
back out, taking care not to wake her,

and as that night-lit child is fully awake the whole
time, with closed eyes, measured breathing,
savoring a delicious blessing she couldn't
name but will remember her whole life,

how often we feel we're being watched over,
or that we're secretly looking in on the ones
we love, even when they are far away,
or even as they are lost in the sleep

no one wakes from—what we know
and what we feel can fully coincide, like love
and worry, like taking care in full silence
and secrecy, like darkness and light together.

Posters the Sun Is Erasing

Nine months missing, stolen from the clear center
of a midwestern parking lot, she smiles
from store windows, church bulletin boards,
the odd car bumper or library checkout.
Faded to cluelessness. The bloodhounds and psychics
have long since retired to fresher mysteries.
The dredged ponds are silting in. Those canisters
for spare change at every convenience store
now gone or pushed back for snack food and lottery.

Only those who knew her still pay the interest
on her vanishing, this cheery woman with
two different haircuts. She'll never headline again
unless she's found, and only a handful of the devout
can still pray in that faith. As sun steadily bleaches
all away, even her winning grin will evaporate
like dew from midmorning asphalt.
No one wants to be first to tear down this image
from the civic mind, so she wanes
indecently, in plain view, until her dumb
and generous mystery shall exactly match our own.

The Turning

—to Jean, one year dead

> *For some time, though, he struggled for more to hold on to. "Are you*
> *sure you have told me everything you know about his death?" he*
> *asked. I said, "Everything." "It's not much, is it?" "No," I replied,*
> *"but you can love completely without complete understanding."*
> —Norman Maclean, *A River Runs Through It*

A year since I drove the thousand miles
it took to face your death. You were dust
before I got there, little different
from grit in the interstate wind,
ashpits smoking in backyards, rest stop tiles
smeared with grease and cracker crumbs.
You were ashes in a box, pills in the trash.

The trance of wheel-hum turned
and turned me away from that day,
away from the moonclear night
with its starry jazz, the glow
of emptied parking lots in Akron
and Youngstown. Turned me again
through thirty years of glimpse
and shrug, angers out of nowhere,
laughter equally so—yet brought me
no closer to you for all
the circus-swirl in my head.

Radio static resolved, near Harrisburg,
to your favorite melody—ice
on my tongue, fire in the blood.
I always thought there would be time
for one more pot simmering

on the stove, one more midnight
cracked open like a beer. Your
last words: "I'll call you right back."

A year now. Why should this May
astonish more or less than your last?
The trillium's up, lilacs and apple blossoms
fading fast, goldfinches stitching
the air tight. We knew summer
would come, then fall's brisk business,
winter with its bleached light,
now spring again in its watery glints,
its bluejay blare trumpeting summer.

We always knew the great mud-
and jewel-encrusted wheel
would roll us away from you, by day,
by season, by year—knew it well
before your bones consumed themselves
and your soul lapsed into morphine coma,
vegetal breath. We couldn't know
the strangeness of the turning.

The odd blessing of meals with
the gathered clan: you would have
savored that kitchen clamor, delicious
choice of side dish and placemat, reels
or ragas to throb in the background.
Heavy mugs lifted in storied air—you
would have giggled at the surge and lilt
of accents, your Dublin brother-in-law
all dickied up like the dog's dinner, a cousin
mad for Cheetos. You would have flit
from kitchen to porch with a fresh bowl
of dip, and said very little.
Well, you're silent now. But no more so

this year than some others I could name.
Now we'll never finish the six-year quarrel
your cancer interrupted without resolving.
That mystery burned with your bones.
Even unto death you preferred
your chatter practical, chemo cocktails,
CAT scans and bloodwork, all the apparatus
of hope, forgive me, without its soul.

I know if you could hear these words
you would swirl away like a scatter
of petals in the wind. How little
your death has changed that. Did the wheel
turn less heavily for you at that
still point? Would you cry to see
your sister cry, slipping on your coat
now washed clean of your scent?
Nothing's ever over.

Today the crows in cemetery treetops
harangue the mowers below, readying
the plots for Memorial Day. Yesterday
workmen hosed poison over the too-lush grass,
and all the dandelions wilted and withered.
I know the turning facts all too well—
gravestones will weather smooth in time,
will crack and crumble to dust, but the weeds
turn up each year brighter than flame.

Summons

The whole time we slept
raccoons stretched and batted
like dreamy cats on our roof.
Not five feet from our pillow
they gamboled, scritching the shingles,
brushing our windowscreen
with ardent fur. Dew-christened
aerialists, they might as well
have sprouted from the dark
like sudden mushrooms, or dropped
on our porch roof by the moon.

I had no need to see
by their ironic masks
what they might think of our married
slumber, side by side like chunks
of firewood, while in the bright
spring air and moonwash this pair
frisked for their own cloudy benefit.

By the time the dog roused us
with his strangled growl, on point
before our common window,
I knew without a glance
what my flashlight would reveal
hissing and humming near at hand—
what else but love itself
somersaulting its antic way
all over our mended roof?

Splash

—in memory of Bob Bradbury

Boys will chuck the heaviest rocks possible
into the smallest streams. Boys live most
in that ka-thunk, that knee-high splatter-splash.
Boys live most in the splintery creak and release
of dead tree at cliff's edge, finally letting loose
its century-hold and taking down its portion of sky
with a worldly crash, down the long scree slope.
Boys live most in the fuse of ashcan, cherry bomb,
M-80 as they sputter and flare toward that satisfying
gut punch sound, that flash, that flame, that
acrid sulfur smell that has a boy's name scrawled
all over it. If no fire is available, a boy will settle
for jackknifing balloons, detonating puffballs
in the woods, beheading wildflowers with
a stripped willow whip-stick. Even at age 66,
walking his aging dog down a winter-gray sidewalk,
a man will kick an ice clod ahead of him
for a full block, and live a while more in that.

Feedback

Like every dipshit faded mill town
we're Historical, news we've posted
on both main roads at the town limits,

but even if paint weren't faded,
you'd know it from potshot rust holes
pocking those signs. You'd know it by

vegetable stands with no produce
at this time, yard dogs lying flat as rugs
as you cruise down Main, vague smell

of hog shit drifting in from the west,
single radio tower blinking its endless
SOS near a driveway curving into

a bald spot in the weeds. You'd know it
from free kittens in a box, Gravel Fill
4 Sale, and this tattoo parlor married

uneasily to the Tae Kwon Do studio.
One cop home for lunch has parked
his patrol car in the yard. His toolshed

out back's older than the house,
leaning hard toward a black-and-white
world, in which Local Couple Celebrates

Sixtieth Wedding Anniversary, with
a photo of two startled youngsters
in front of a grainy, washed-out lilac,

both frowning as if they might
at any moment maybe grin—
but if that moment ever came, it went,

down into the church basement
with casserole dishes and fluorescents
humming, margarine tubs on every

table holding down paper tablecloths,
the hiss of ancient radiators, and thick
smell of damp wool. Meanwhile,

up in his bedroom, everyone's little
brother practices guitar as loudly as he
dares, feedback pouring from cheap amp—

probably still not loud enough for him,
because if Mom hears him over her TV,
she'll shout *Pipe down!* and he will.

Junk Shop Shadows

I like the idea of junk shops more than
being in one—the dust and clutter,
renegade odors of failure and loss,
the sag in the shoulders of someone's
old wedding suit. Nothing lasts,
and not a soul scrawling their chipper
weather reports in these racks
of sun-faded postcards has the slightest
idea. It's the smell of almost successful
air fresheners, shadows between
the aisles mumbling and coughing softly.

So what's to like? That you can
almost see how every miserable
doo-dad was once someone's
luminous dream. I like how no one
pretends to have a plan, but just
shuffles one day to the next
in comfortable shoes. The impossible
abundance of the past, like a kettle
of soup before you ladle out
the first bowl. That long moment
when everything is still delicious.

Nursing Home

How like a museum these rooms appear:
peering in at doorways, you see briefest echo
or facsimile—photos, a small shelf of books,

well worn easy chair. Not nearly enough
to liven these carpetless rooms. Even the residents
look abstracted, their own thumbed-through artifacts,

and it takes patience to guide them
through their mumblings, their glazed insistences.
And many so sick they merely exist,

as if their stones were already carved.
Traveler, pass by! So you do, not wanting
to provoke weary bones before they're well planted.

You think: all I want is to die at home, amid more
than wisps and tokens of who I am. You think:
who among these shades did not wish the same?

Homage To Sadie Bosheers

Sadie, you gave me this shirt on my back,
tested my wayward seams and tugged my buttons
long before I knew I would clothe myself
in your care. So I wanted you to know
I keep your cryptic message, "Inspected
by Sadie Bosheers," in a little teak box
on my desk, along with a Canadian coin
and one of my dog's puppy teeth.

I save it as oracle, this slip of paper
no bigger than my favorite
cookie fortune: "You are doomed
to be happy in wedlock." It's true
I'm doomed, Sadie, and I like to think
you might still find me happy enough,
though my elbows have begun to poke
through sleeves you certified so long ago.

Your signature is printed, not handwritten,
which to me just increases
your impartial grace. You had no need
to boast or qualify, just put down
one firm line to say that Sadie Bosheers
was here, on the job, living the life.
It's no statement about the honor
of hard toil, no suave calling card,
no complaint I read in your message.

Still, I accept the odd opaque blessing
of Sadie Bosheers—you step out calmly,
robed only in your own name, and meet
my dumb gaze. I pronounce that name,

and feel our separate dooms merge
in common air, both duly inspected,
both found somehow acceptable on this earth.

II

Long Overdue Note to My College Professor Who Broke Down and Cried One Morning in 1974 While Teaching Yeats

At long last I know what you mean.
That was no country for any man,
that classroom with its fluorescent rows
of groggy juniors equal in fear

and indifference. We were in
no one's arms but yours, and you split
open like a shell to reveal
the raw jelly inside. We froze,

thinking it was family woe,
maybe an old back injury
acting up, perhaps even fear
of tenure's blank guillotine.

Maybe so, maybe so. Now I
think it was us, our practiced slouch,
our gaze blank and pitiless as
the clock itching toward hour's end.

We weren't about to appreciate Yeats
on your say-so. We were thinking
grades, thinking lunch, thinking firelight
playing upon a girlfriend's skin,

and we were thinking them so hard
we couldn't feel what you said
Yeats felt. So in piteous rage
at our held breaths, our cautious nods,

you wept. And we didn't know how
to be anything but polite
about it. You stammered, halted,
and stood bent over the lectern

in pain. We studied our notes. We
glanced at the swaying trees outside
while you cried silently into,
over, and about our silence.

David Divides His Time

David Graham does not divide his time
between Nantucket and Chicago,
or between his childhood farm
and his condo on Maui or Oahu.

Nevertheless, he does divide his time
between office computer
and home machine, sometimes
sending email from one to the other.

He divides his time between boyhood
and a generalized woozy fog,
between known and unknown,
between lakewater and a modest mountain
rising into Adirondack clouds.

David divides his time ruthlessly,
recklessly, eagerly, like a dog on a scent,
and like the spaniel in his field
when the scent dwindles to nothing.

He often divides his time badly,
always with some left over—
too small a portion to use,
too great to just toss away.

Sometimes David wishes
to divide his time more ways,
like a chess master circling the room,
unsatisfied with one, two, three
victories, moving on, going for the record.

Other times, he wishes his time
could grow even more singular,
contracting to a mug of fresh coffee
at the kitchen table, radio playing Bach,
and no interruptions the entire morning.

Mostly he divides his time without
realizing. He took a shortcut home
one day in his thirty-fourth year,
and arrived at age sixty-three somehow
on the same tank of gas. Beard gray
and no clear map in his head.

David divides his time between
the San Francisco of memory
and the London of imagination,
the Walden Pond without bottom
and the marriage bed on which
he's floated for decades now
upon the darkest water.

But when the alarm goes off
he's sitting in traffic, dividing
his time between left turn and
no turn at all. Or maybe not.
His mind divides on the question.

Why I Love America

Like America, I love having reasons I don't need,
like I love the smell of American bubblegum
and the imperial amazement of interstates
—we invented interstates, world!—

and of course I love blues and jazz
and Charles Ives and his crazy fedora,
not to mention Abe Lincoln and Ray Charles
—we created Abe and Ray!—

I love how we take everybody in
and *make* them American if need be,
from Charlie Chaplin to Bob Hope and Neil Young
—and we have the best Cary Grants in the world!—

I love how even when I'm not paying attention
baseball is being played, seriously, in America,
played by Dominican, Japanese, and Cuban guys
—the world is nuts about our baseball!—

Needless to say I adore bluegrass
and pale watery beer, wine by the tanker truck
bound for every supermarket, wine so cheap
even I can pretend to be a snob!

The only country where Bob Dylan and
Johnny Cash could get famous and rich—as *singers*!
We like scruffy, ragged, whiny voices in America
—the kind of scratchy voice Whitman had!—

I love skateboards, Motown, self-serve gas,
the Outer Banks, and a certain mountain valley

in Virginia filling at dusk with fireflies
—do they even have fireflies in Egypt? Mexico?—

I love the Constitution, Langston Hughes,
the Tappan Zee, Macintoshes whether fruit
or computer, Dolly Parton, Huck Finn
—put Dolly anywhere else, she'd vanish—

I love that Ben Franklin invented the glasses
I'm wearing, that he started a lending library
and even now appears on the hundred dollar bill
—and isn't it great how we can call him Ben?—

You may wonder just how sappy I can get,
if there's anything I *don't* love about America,
and I will probably just stare back at you
from under my baseball cap, wondering

if I'm truly a sap or you're an idiot for asking
—the answer is *of course I'm a sap, you idiot*, but
truth is I hate America just as much as you
—Granddad America spouting racist nonsense—

and there is *always* a need to hate Wounded Knee,
Vietnam, Selma, Jackson State and Kent State,
"separate but equal," Guantanamo, Trail of Tears,
but if all you ever do is name Hiroshima and not

"I Have a Dream," always "Relocation Centers"
and never "West End Blues," you risk thinking
that's all, and anyway it's all being swept
down the big muddy along with Ty Cobb and Scott Joplin

and even old Andrew Carnegie, that heartless,
penny-pinching Scot that America transformed
into a philanthropist at the end

—thank you, Andrew, for my hometown library!
So thank you, America, for being big enough
to take in all praise and all blame, sin and glory,
without filling up, as the Mississippi and Hudson
run into the sea, and yet the sea is not full.

"Thou May'st in Me Behold"

Look at this man at his window all agog
at the mortal weather. Fall's doing its misty thing,
leaves swirling to the ground, and most of us,
it seems, are a little past our sell-by dates.

Comfort comes in various guises,
like the soft grandmotherly hands of day
rolling you back to sleep after night frost.
Or: not like that at all: it depends

on factors like how many dead flies per sill,
how bright the stars, where do clouds go
when midnight moon shines its spot—
To love that well which thou must leave ere long?

Well, kind of. Mostly it's the slow quilt
slipping to the floor somehow in the night,
and running after it in time-lapse dreams,
sleet ticking on your face like rice thrown at a bride.

Ode to the Faces in Renaissance Paintings

I do delight in the sneers, the dirty-nailed hands
clutching Bibles, five o'clock shadow
faithfully rendered. I believe in stringy hair
no cap can tame: all flesh is grass, etcetera.
And sumptuous gowns, architectural hats,
ermine and tooled leather—all that extravagance
in stark contrast to the skeleton lurking behind
the drapes, or a skull glowing on the table
next to a tipped-over globe. Even Adam
and Eve, stripped to their shame, look like
our next door neighbors as they hustle
away down the path toward our smelly world.

It's great how these folks lust and sweat
and squint in irritation, so unlike rococo saints
in the next gallery, those spirits purged
in advance of all fleshly delight
and earthly burden, their haloed skin
stretched and burnished by no light I've
ever seen. *These* lords and ladies jowly
and multi-chinned, wrinkled, hawk-nosed
and wary-eyed. As well they should be,
now five centuries and more since death,
stared at and judged and subjected
to monographs disputing even their names.

This man, a butcher from next door
to the painter's studio, sported a halo
and bogus scriptural identity by the time
the first paint dried. But X-ray analysis
was hardly needed to put the lie to such
nonsense: this lined face with its beard stubble

and warm-beer flush was never anything
but one of us, gassy and exasperated
as the long seconds of the pose ticked by.

I seek such faces in the crowds behind
each miracle or martyrdom, faces
from grocery store and bus stop, gawkers
at a house fire, fans in the bleachers, faces
I know and thus can believe, with their
shifty looks and well-lined brows
somehow undissolved by time, not a miracle
but close enough for this believer.

As the Sun Says

I like to think that out in the simmering marshes,
some bird extinct for a hundred or three hundred years

lifts off its nest as usual, flies around as it did
during the Roman Empire, all through the Black Death

and the Crusades, hunting up grubs to gobble down
as it will during the Gilded Age and the surrender

of Sitting Bull, perching, preening, completely oblivious
as always to conquistador, president, CEO, professor,

utterly unaware of its own obituaries in the textbooks,
unconcerned with the very existence of textbooks,

just rising and spreading wing as the sun says
and has always said—for what else do you do?

It isn't even a question, for there are no questions,
and time is not a concept that has a sliver

of the meaning of one rotting stump, rich as always
with ants, beetles, and three kinds of savory worm.

Just Trying to Get to Sandusky, He Said

"I'm not a car jacker or anything," he muttered,
and in truth I believed him. Nothing bad-ass
about his fairly new jeans, yellow polo shirt,
and hair no shaggier than mine. Maybe forty.
Still, he had the sidelong drift of a panhandler
and sure enough out came his pitch: sister
in trouble in Sandusky, and he somehow
without his billfold on the interstate, almost
out of gas and still a hundred miles to go.

I didn't see any car, but passed him a few bucks
to make him go away, which he did without
even a thank-you, leaving me to appreciate
the starkness of our exchange. He didn't pretend
to be grateful, I didn't pretend to believe him.
I don't expect he'll pay it forward, either.

"Best I can do," I shrugged, handing him
the few ones in my wallet, not about to part with
a twenty just to feel the buzz of being that kind
of man. But he was ambling away before I stowed
my billfold back in my pocket—no doubt already
seeking his next sucker or—who knows?—a saint.

For why *wouldn't* a saint ride the Ohio Turnpike
looking to improve the dusty miles between
Cleveland and Toledo? Surely if I were a saint
I would often be found in Vermilion, Lorain,
Elyria and Strongsville. I would know people
in Huron and Wilmer, and yes, would have
a sister in Sandusky.

She would live just off
Grand Avenue of the Republic Highway
and wouldn't have been down to the lake
in years. That's something we talked about—
a picnic at the lake sometime when we weren't
so busy and had some leisure time, some nice
sunset night in July, a trace of autumn cool
in the breeze and a sixpack good and gold
to work on. But then Sandi got so sick,
and it was all I could do to get over there
once every couple-three weeks or so
to help mow the yard and bring a few groceries.

But mostly just to talk, sipping our coffees,
deep talk like we haven't done since we were kids,
and now it seems time might be limited
and anyway, neither of us talks anymore
about heading down to the lake. Maybe that's sad
or maybe, as Sandi would say, it's just realistic,
but in any case, she won't see another sunset
off those waters in this lifetime, and we both
feel it. Can you spare a twenty for *that*, pal?

The Look of a Bay Mare

And the look of a bay mare shames silliness out of me.
—Walt Whitman

Yes, but what about this goofy possum
waddling myopic across my midnight yard?

Compared to that I'm practically full of *gravitas*.

And besides, that old bay mare won't give me
the time of day, runs away from
my generous carrot, my sugar cube.

Still, here I am waiting for The Look to banish
all my folly and absurdity—but perhaps I've got
too much for your average horse to handle.

Ever think of *that*, Walt Whitman?

Maybe it would take a bison at least
to shame the likes of me.

Possibly I'd require all of childhood's blushes
and an entire waning moon to boot.

And what if I *like* my silliness?

Surely you of all people, Walt, would understand
if I kept a little bit of it in my pocket
like hard candy, to be doled out to children

and the variously wounded. You could have filled
the East River with the smallest portion
of your good gray silliness, after all—

That was at least half your charm.

Well, we all waddle across
the dewy grass sometime,
dragging our ropy tails. Why not tonight?

Valentine Despite Valentine's Day

—for Lee

I prance nonchalant amid the sentiments:
fat phony hearts clogging the shopwindows,
red wings flapping up the aisles
and top-forty cupids beaming
like idiot contestants in fluorescent gloss.
Well, their desire's innocent. Unlike mine, which scalds
like an incandescent bulb to your familiar touch.

Maybe passion can withstand
the cash register's ping. Perhaps a mound of candy
really sweetens things—one drug that works.
In this store I spy two lonely swains
fingering the merchandise, both so solemn, love's
very conscripts. I watch them blandly. But for blandness
I'll say this much—married, I suppose, to the common ploys—
it's love I feel, blistering these candied aisles
at the unsimple thought of you.

Crab, Lobsters, Monkfish, Conger Eel, & Squid

I am so glad I'm not Queen, having to display
no spark of irritation while schoolgirls curtsy stiffly,
Irishmen on street corners scowl and drag hard
on their cigarettes as my motorcade passes,
and I must smile and appear politely fascinated
when I am shown "more than forty varieties
of fresh seafood" at the fishmarket, "including
crab, lobsters, monkfish, conger eel, and squid,"
as *The Telegraph* dutifully reports, along with an MP
sneering at such fuss over this "wealthy aristocrat."

I am so glad no one photographs me being assisted
out of my own car or waits in a cold rain
for two hours just for the chance to glimpse me
waving once before I must disappear into
the new youth center for its dedication ceremony.

But even more, I am glad I do not have to listen
to those speeches in my honor, or have someone
close by my side at all times to ensure I am comfortable
and asking if I should like some tea. Sometimes
I like to just wander down the gray sidewalk
with no destination at all, following my dog
as he lazily sniffs the bushes and windblown trash
caught in a chain link fence, and whether or not
I like the cut of the fence, or if I am enjoying
my aimless journey down Thorne Street headed
toward Union, no soul on earth shall inquire.

Black Tea

In her author's photos over the years,
she stays the same age, maybe even
growing a little bit younger.
It's on the page where she keeps aging,

loses two husbands to younger women,
sends a bitter daughter off to college,
holds the dying hand of her father.
Such a huge booming man: his flabby grip

heartbreaking. Or she's back in college herself,
angering Dad by choosing man after man
exactly like him. Now one old boyfriend
sends sweet wistful emails she daydreams over.

But no. The time for nonsense is long gone.
Fierce as a bluejay over her black tea,
pen in hand, she slashes at the page, erasing
that beautiful young woman word by word.

Sand Against the Wind

Mock on, mock on, Voltaire, Rousseau;
Mock on, mock on; 'tis all in vain!
You throw the sand against the wind,
And the wind blows it back again.
          —William Blake

As even turtles know, sunning themselves
on an afternoon rock in the barely moving
stream, there are only so many hours

in a day. Yes, and only so many years
in a life, though that's perhaps beyond
a turtle's ken—who can say for sure?—

but surely there's not much excuse
for the likes of me spending
one more hot minute online, scanning

the vids and memes, political outrage,
traveling vicariously to the Grand Canyon
or blue Danube, witnessing

many a flash-blasted plate of pasta
and a richness of rickety smiles.
And there's definitely no reason

to read, much less share, a Facebook
post mocking some hapless soul
who doesn't know how to spell "cologne"—

as in, "When he passed by, I was
intoxicated by the smell of his colon."
Which is funny, sure, but just reminds us

how paltry a thing is mockery,
how poisonous and soul-deadening,
unless perhaps directed at the rich

or powerful in their eternal pomposity—
but even then it's risky, for the mocker
can easily confuse ridicule with wisdom

or virtue, which is itself a mockable offense.
Better to just feel sun warm your shell for
as long as you can, then plop back in the pond.

Vinegar and Fizz

I.

My mother could not be trusted
to tell it straight. She adored welshing
on a bet, spinning tales, splashing
in hyperbole's lake. Relished a circus,
the bellow and roar, musk and glitter,
bananas vanishing down clown pants
in cheap yellow air. First in line for
the freak show, dazzled by carny patter.
Never met a dog or horse she didn't
love. Children, maybe yes, maybe no.
She spoke other languages if possible,
applied pressure to a bleeding wound,
plucked floundering toddlers out of
the deep end, getting her good
house dress soaked. You wanted her
around in an emergency. But what
an unreliable witness! She told it slant,
but never all. *Couldn't* tell it straight,
I think, but when have facts ever been
the point of any tale? Don't bet against
her, friend. Did her many balloons wobble
brightly to the ceiling? Yes. Did she
place a single peanut on my pudgy
palm for the elephant to lift with its
trunk? Of course. A touch still zapping
me sixty years later. My mother would
never turn away from any elephant,
juggler, parade, song, or barker
beating his drum of gorgeous lies.

2.

The doctor settles opposite her in a straight chair
looking kindly and earnest, and I can tell
what's coming. He asks her her name
and of course she snorts, "You know *that!*"
Yes, he does. But then he inquires if she can say
what season. She looks around the ward
craftily: decorated tree, tinsel, cartoon snowflakes
stuck to the windows. "It's almost Christmas.
What are you getting me?" Next he wonders
if she knows the year. She glares into his face,
allows a sullen pause. . . . Then, "1937," she says.

And so it is. She's going on sixteen, a girl
ready to burn and roam, nobody's fool,
a spitfire, all vinegar and fizz. The War
is but a vague mist on the horizon. This year
has a gleaming, sun-scoured sound. 1937.
The train is about to leave the station
for the one and only time. She'll be damned
if she won't be on it, and ride far from home.

The Crow from Home

It is the crow from home
that cawed above the immense
gaunt bear eating sweet-pea vines
and wild strawberries.
　　　—Jim Harrison

In morning's maple it is the crow
from home, hunched cackling
on a bare branch as usual,
all disdain and dismissal
just as in 1963, when I labored
up the drive in my snow suit,
a laughable puff of nothing
yet utterly earthbound, sweaty
and pale. And silhouetted
atop a flagless pole as dusk rose
like a river over the deserted
playing fields of Hanover, NH
in 1974, where I walked
and walked my mind blank
as the snowy streets. I knew
that crow also. Same shape
perched on a nearby tombstone
when I poured ashes into
a fresh hole in 2001—not even
an omen, just a torn-off scrap
of night on morning's lawn.
That black shape also crossed
in front of my car when I drove
down Switzer Hill one last time,
fishtailing, going too fast
in the freezing rain, yet it seems
we both made it from dark
to dark. Whether bent over
road kill, picking scraps from

the dumpster, flying alone
at twilight over a bare corn field,
that crow from home finally
has nothing in its beak
but the sound of a rusty
door-hinge in the wind, and
nothing to do but swoop low
over me as if in attack,
then up to a roadside pine
landing light as a shadow.

Thanksgiving Snow

It's like living with ghosts, Mary says,
her parents walking and talking with her daily.
Lee says, *I think of Jeannie all the time—*
our newest ghost this Thanksgiving.

This is what old friends do for holiday:
sip wine and add up the losses,
grow still as evening chills and deepens.
I don't remember my parents, when they were

our age, says Mary, *complaining this much.*
Lee says, *Maybe they simply didn't let us
hear it.* A new bottle of Merlot to that.
Billie Holiday's voice rising as ours fall.

We've been friends well over half a lifetime.
And this *is* a life: dog snoring on the carpet,
art on every wall, candles guttering—
but we've got more, as we've got more to say,

though not tonight, slowed with good bread
and soup, getting tired, no alarm clock
in the morning, no journey to embark on,
no appointment or ceremony beyond

the slow feast we'll make of the whole
blessed day. Colder by morning, a few
snowflakes drifting, not like ghosts, not like
words freed from meaning. Just flakes in the air.

Letters from the Dead

Mostly it's all jabber and babble, chaff
pouring off the yellowed pages,
jaunty quips and pro forma feelings.
So sorry not to write sooner, they say,

and you can see they are unsorry as cats,
these long-vanished voices gathered now
in shoeboxes, bound by stiff rubber bands.
They're so unaware of the grinding gears

of time, you have to stop reading,
rise on creaky knees from the closet,
and look out the window for a minute
at dusk collecting in the blue spruce.

Well, it was a lot of fun, they report,
just back from Bimini or Holland,
leaving no record of any actual fun, already
fretting about falling behind at work.

They say *saw this article and thought of you*,
though the clipping long since fell out
and you don't recognize the handwriting.
Someone, somewhere, sometime

thought of you. No news of impending
death, or religious terror, or
the finely milled sadness of life. No,
they are looking forward to the new job,

first grandchild, upcoming move to Tampa,
and at most they're uneasily ironic
about the hurricanes that will sweep
their coastlines and upend all the trees.

We would die laughing if it were funny,
if it were not our hands opening
those dusty envelopes, our shelves
we pile the letters on—to be reread

later, when we're better able to face it,
when things will be a little less crazy
around here, after we're back from Bimini
or Holland, and able at last to relax.

For no one ever writes *goodbye, this is it*,
even near the palpable end. They write
more later, I'm tired now, and these
are the words we must carve on their stones.

The Pump Handle

I like coming upon little bits of art
in woods or fields. The tiniest signs
of a human hand shaping, making.
Garland of grasses woven and left
by the creek. Twig figure standing
watch in the crotch of a box elder.
Smiley face sketched in fresh-fallen
snow. *Curt + Libby 4EVR* carved
on a beech trunk, now fallen
and slowly closing over with moss.

Even just a small stone centered
atop a larger. Anything that says
I was here, which is plenty to say
in this eroding world. So I was
sad to see the rusty old pump
in the middle of my favorite woods
had finally lost its handle, fallen
or torn off its pipe to join the duff,
or maybe carried off by kids.

The farm it watered long gone
even before I was born. But I've
marked the spot for thirty years
of hikes in all weathers, all
the while thinking of brothers
called in to supper, Holsteins
crowding up to the trough, some
mother humming her hymns
as the pump squealed
and gushed day after day.

Which Is to Say

Now that I'm old, I'm oddly
nostalgic not for childhood
but for my thirties,
which is to say, it's all
a little fuzz-edged now,
where we lived, how it felt,
what we said to our
thirty-something pals
at those long parties we'd
throw, everyone all glistening,
getting gin-and-tonic'd
out on the unburned lawn,
maybe some sweaty volleyball
or frisbee, for we were quite
young, which is to say,
we felt old. We'd stock
each other's fridges with
Carlo Rossi and Old Milwaukee.
We'd live on nuts and chips.
Sure, we'd wake all cottony
and throbbing, but that was
a sign of intensity. Our bones
were strong. Which is to say,
they were not. We maybe
guzzled too much too often
for clearly remembering
how great it was to be
thirty-something, with, yes,
the yearning urgent flesh,
and of course some major
flirtation, not all of it harmless.
Which is to say, there were
long, loud, torn-scab breakups,

there was shrieking in
backseats and bedrooms,
which is to say, we mostly
lost one half of each
breaking-up couple, you had
to choose, you needed to say
wise and sympathetic things,
but only to her, or only to him.
You had to vote. And once you've
sat handing tissues to a grown
man who hasn't left your sofa
for three days straight, and heard
of every kinky regrettable thing,
well, you get a bit weary,
which is to say, you remember
all this imperfectly at best,
this rosy amorphous feeling now
being a vast oversimplification
based on the inscrutable
holy mystery of time, and yes,
perhaps a tad more vodka
than was strictly helpful.
So those were not simpler
times, not happier, they were
just thirty-something years
ago, which is to say, precious
as any lost gem or bent key.

"How Would Jesus Drive?"

—*painted on a truck, Ohio Turnpike*

Well, there would be no road rage, that's for sure.
Smoothly shifting down the entrance ramps,
never hogging the passing lane or driving
twenty miles with his left blinker on,
he would wave joyfully to kids in passing cars,
he would leave clear dry road behind
even in the worst sleet storm or blizzard.

In truth, he would be a bit of a pain in the butt,
lingering forever at intersections, letting others
go first, stopping motorists to alert them
to better driving techniques, announcing
to the big-rig drivers at the truckstop
that they should all abandon their loads
immediately, pile in his van for the long haul
to salvation—

                leaving those eighteen-wheelers
with emptied cabs in the parking lot,
rumbling as they spew diesel exhaust
into the sinful air, all their cargoes
of milk or oranges slowly going bad.

Heaven Changes

Sure, you might find him up at three
But if he is it's just to pee.
    —Loudon Wainwright III

How when young we spoke
in the morning of party antics
the night before, who said and did
and how much and what and oh no,

but these days it's how well
or ill we slept, the grail being
seven or even eight straight hours
with no bathroom shuffle-dance

or existential vagueness for an hour
after three, and of course waking
at all, good heavens, and stepping
down on rug with minimal pain,

yes, heaven changes as you approach,
like a rainbow glistening in a field
toward which the young girl
gallops in joy of first touching

such magic, while we, who may
or may not have slept soundly
last night, watch her running
with noncommittal smiles,

in fact watching for that moment
we know is coming, when
the rainbow in all its glory
just vanishes, gone in a blink,

and there she stands, breathless
in the middle of a rain-dazzled
hay field, looking around and around
for wherever it could have gone.

Small Round Valentine

—*on our anniversary*

Everything is curve and circle,
rondure, swell and dip and eddy,
everything, even in the sky,
wheels and turns, and the earth
orbits, and the moon,

and the water in its bed
flows in graceful curves
on its way to return, return,
as the seasons return,

and the night, and every thought
worth having, like a fine meal
prepared and rounded out
by love's hand,

like music searching
its final chord, like once
upon a time again, again,

like your body quickening
to my simple hand.

At Sixty-Five

On my birthday I want nothing but
more of everything. More damn snow,
more coffee jitters, more wind fluting
down the chimney insanely. More news
to sigh and shake my head over. I want
a little salt and pepper to taste, and more
if I feel like it. More walks in the woods
with my lifetime sweet one, counting deer
as the owl counts us. More time than
a dog has, more than we need or deserve.
And when the larder is full, the bed
brimful with easy flow, air electric
with all air brings and every sign
on the road leads to repletion and
plenty and copious fullness, then,
then I say more. *I say more.*

I Dream of Jeannie

Coming in the door after walking the dog,
glasses fogged solid, untangling glove and leash,

I'm slow to realize it's not Lee on the couch
but Jeannie. "I've come for a *visit!*" she cries,

all smiles and looking just as she did
in about 1978. No chemo hair, no bloating,

no limp, no broken ribs from chemo-weak bones—
all that is either long in the future

or else the past. I'm not sure of the rules here.
And she's not going to help me understand,

but when did she ever? She's all giggly, though,
just as of old, and it takes me a while more

to see it's over the man she's brought along—
not Damian or anyone I've ever met,

but a nice curly-headed guy with sly grin.
He's about her age, and I can see him

as one of those guys everyone likes right off
because he laughs at jokes and never challenges

anyone. I immediately like him, too,
though he just stares and doesn't give a peep,

and she just giggles more, and I wake
inconclusively, which seems about right.

Pale Blues

—the night I skipped Duke Ellington

The suave one, already sick and months away
from death, would have loved me madly
had I shown, even in my silly bellbottoms,
my scruffy parka, my contempt for an elegance
forged from more than a white tuxedo.
Johnny Hodges and Billy Strayhorn dead,
Ben Webster long gone—it was nothing
like the glitter of 1941, but no matter:
had it been the Cotton Club and not
icy New Hampshire, I wouldn't have heard
a thing. I lounged in my room no more than
a hundred yards from the theater,
amped up on some pale boy blues
long melted from my mind like the flurries
crossing my sill that night forty years ago.

Had I shown he might have hit a riff, though,
to lift even me a few inches out of my seat,
some chord so blue I could taste it.
But I knew without knowing in those days.
I was the star, the moon, the wheeling night
above Smarts Mountain. I did not need
that dapper genius showing me anything
about the music of the spheres.

Walking to the snack bar later, I saw
the tour bus grumbling in winter air,
stooped black men loading instrument cases,
and I did not pause to see if I might recognize
his weary face, those famous sagging eyes,
or if perhaps he was already racing in a solo car

down I-91, the gig well gone from his mind,
some scrap of new rhythm seeming
to rise from the drone of tires,
the tiny squeal of wind in the side vents.

Tim's Tale

These faded little towns you drive through
in Georgia, Ohio, Minnesota, the hills
of western Pennsylvania, upstate New York—

every one looks about the same to you
with its seedy auto body shop, full graveyard,
its three churches and seven bars,

not to mention the shuttered department store,
big old houses that've seen better days,
and vacant lots where something or other

burned down years ago—the scent
of soot still rises after every rain or snow.
But you know if you just coasted to a stop

in front of the 7-Eleven, got out of your
car and strolled the three-block
Main Street, you'd begin to notice things.

Three-legged white cat scampering up
some porch steps. The sign over the River
View Diner, when light hits it just so,

revealing it used to be The Majestic.
Skinny boy in his driveway practicing
layups—most beautiful shots you've ever seen.

Then some guy with the name of Tim
embroidered in red on his work shirt
looking and looking at you in the Walgreen's

where you've stopped for some aspirin
and a soda. He's staring so hard because
surely you remind him of someone

he went to school with, but hasn't seen
in forty-five years—moved to Texas, he
heard, but after all this time, who knows?

He's trying to decide whether or not to
greet you with your old name, while
you ponder whether or not you'll accept it,

or just shake your head and turn away.

"Most of the Time We Live Through the Night"

—Robert Bly

Most of the time the dark waters will rise,
then fall into sun and birdsong, everything
glistening, vivid as broken glass in fresh mud.
Most of the time the dire phone does not ring,

your brakes hold firm, fever breaks, letter arrives
in plenty of time with the full amount enclosed.
Most of the time when we speak our love
we mean it. When you walk the winter cemetery

and fifty crows lift off at once from a bare oak,
most of the time it portends nothing at all.
Just a bit of dust moving around the universe.
Just another omen that means nothing, really,

but what water means flowing over the stones
in the creek. Most of the time Sunday has
little to tell Saturday night, and almost nothing
Monday morning needs to hear. *The best days*

are the first to flee, Virgil told us long ago,
but we didn't listen, did we? We ran through
summer grass and winter snow, and most
of the time that was just the right thing to do.

To Judge the Sky

Poor earth, that dare presume to judge the sky.
—Fulke Greville

Poor knobby-kneed humans with soup stained shirts
and lottery tickets in your wallets like cancelled stamps.
Imagine having brand loyalty and a favorite sit-com.
Poor dirt clods aspiring to join the jet stream.

That thud you just heard on the porch?
It was the mailman falling on his face laughing:
something about your bills. Or perhaps it was
some vital part of your past breaking off at last.

Poor mind showing its homemade videos to itself
all night long. And re-runs to boot. Poor pride
ashamed of itself, and with good reason. Poor sax solo
that outran its own end, and so cannot stop now.

Poor cloud wishing to become a stone, while the stone,
of course, yearns to be cloud. Poor everyman in Everytown—
we cannot thank you enough for your balloon dreams
rising above the aerials as if up were just the reasonable way.

What the Deranged Old Woman at the Laundromat Said When I Wasn't Listening

You don't know me, not one little bit,
with your big eyes like river stones
pulled up to dull in the sunlight.

I've seen lots of men like you,
flycasting into the dirt of your driveways.
Then hang limp like a flag with no wind.

I'll bet there are dollar bills in your wallet
haven't seen daylight for years.
I can smell it from here. If I were to cut

into your pasty skin with this purse knife
I know only dust would come out,
maybe some old gray pillowfeathers.

Offer to drive me home. It's obvious
you're thinking about it. How I would look
climbing up the wooden steps ahead.

How I just stare at a dog once
and he turns tail and runs. How
it didn't take a jukebox or a paycheck,

either one, to get me here. You think you
know me? I've been simmering since before
you were born. Won't take much till I boil.

Ode to Baraboo, Wisconsin

"The 54th Best Small Town in the Nation"
—road sign outside Baraboo, Wisconsin

You have to love a town for a brag
so elastic and middle-aged.
You could live 53 lifetimes
in a better place than Baraboo,
as even Baraboo has to admit,
and if you're looking for fine food
or a decent bookstore, if you hanker
to dwell in celestial single digits,
well, you'll need to rise
considerably higher on the list.

And if you seek a place
that is not satellite to some other,
maybe you'll settle in Chicago,
the second or third best metropolis,
or possibly Cleveland, the sixth most
misunderstood. Or head straight
to Pittsburgh, the single most likely
to feature in cop movie chase scenes
in need of big abandoned factories. . .

Plenty of other small towns, lost
in the triple digits, advance their own
decent claims: my Johnstown,
New York, remains the former
glove capital of the world, main
contributor to the tenth most
polluted creek, and forever
most apt to provoke visitors
into saying, "Isn't this where
they had the big flood?"

But Baraboo is sticking to its guns,
and you have to admire their faith
stretched so thinly down to the dozens,
reaching for that statistical heaven
where all places excel. You have to value
a place that knows its limitations
without giving an inch
to the competition—wily Auburn,
Massachusetts, at number 55,
or ambitious Christiansburg, Virginia,
temporarily stalled at 56
because some high school kids
just TP'd the Baptist church—but still
a great town, they're not afraid to tell you,
wonderful place to raise children...

I'm not one to judge, of course,
being merely the ten-thousand-eleventh
best poet in the universe, but
apparently I'm the very first
to happen upon Baraboo, Wisconsin's
shining truth. Imagine—to be not merely
the circus capital of the land, not simply
home to the International Crane Foundation—
but one very good place for birds,
clowns, and poets to gather up
and count their dozens of blessings.

A Wineglass Full of Nails

All night he scuffles bedroom to bathroom to pantry,
searches the faces on the refrigerator,
pill schedules and emergency numbers.
Shuffles on big careful feet to the sink,
where a notepad gives him the name of his
daughter, here for a visit. Midnight. He shakes
the door locks. Grabs a cookie, perhaps.
One o'clock. Swivels the thermostat to ninety.
One-thirty. Adds a log to the wood stove.
Runs water, then leaves it going while he looks
in the den for a glass. Two a.m. Three.

Each night some minor surrealism:
Sofa cushions jammed in the closet, maybe,
or jumper cables in the tub soaking.
On top of the TV, like dried flowers,
a wineglass full of nails. Whatever he seeks
isn't here anymore, yet he paces
like a prisoner, still aimed and active.

These nightly wanderings must be all inkling,
all shadow and itch. Every morning he announces
it's time to head home. Now, though, he just
unplugs a couple lamps. Shelves a book backwards.
Scuffs to the door to check the locks again.

In Line at the Post Office

Here comes a woman with one of those helmet hairdos,
a lacquered orange *objet* of stunning ugliness
riding her head, a petrochemical mote in my eye —
so I stare and stare like a toddler until good grace kicks in.
This scene could go two ways, and thank the wind
it is the sun filling my eyes next, not grit or tears
of derision, and I nod politely, a smalltown St. Francis
here on the mottled official stone, here under
the dazzling commemorative posters, and just two steps
from a limp flag. Bless us all, I'm thinking,
in our transparent disguises, bless our skinny thoughts
escaping this grungy world far and wide.

New Year Love

Forty-four years since I first read,
on a ten-below New Year's Eve,
the thousand year old complaint of Tu Fu:
I brood on the uselessness of letters.

The house crackled with abiding cold.
I lay in a borrowed bedroom, feeling
keenly the strangeness of its settlings.
Wind at the windows startled me

into hearing the *skritch* of my own pen.
It was a love poem I labored over,
long lost now, along with dozens more
melted like frost skimming the morning pane.

I put aside that stiff and useless lyric
and paged through Tu Fu until the flurries
in my head quieted to a solemn clarity.
Useless letters: I do not wish

to lecture that boy now, though if I could
I'd nudge him next door, to the bedroom
where his dear one lay sleeping, and sleeps now,
four decades later, while snow teases the pane.

The Honey of Earth

The honey of heaven may or may not come,
But that of earth both comes and goes at once.
　　　　　—Wallace Stevens

We wake to winter blaze on our windows—
the world whitened while we slept
through gray-brown weeks
of rotten nutfall and littering leaves
crusted with ice. We rise like fever
against frost skimming the pane, we rise burning
and pure as the clouds piling our back yard.
If this isn't our valentine, what is?
We'll scrawl this newly-blank slate like kids
and erase at leisure. The world loves us,
we say, the world loves us not. Solve for X,
the flurries mumble, settling down to stay.
Beneath the tumble and flutter of snow
lie bulbs stored in ice-lock, ready to burn
and shudder upward from their own decay,
the honey of earth immemorial.
So I send you this valentine, though it comes
and goes at once, though it kites
like a snowflake up and down, over and out.

Acknowledgments

Deepest thanks to the editors of the following publications, where many of these poems appeared previously, sometimes in earlier versions:

Cortland Review: "David Graham, Or Current Resident," "Homage to Sadie Bosheers"

Eclectica: "The Turning," "Ode to Baraboo, Wisconsin"

Famous Reporter: "Summons"

Linebreak: "Thou May'st in Me Behold"

Live Encounters: "Junk Shop Shadows," "Sand Against the Wind"

One: "What the Deranged Old Woman at the Laundromat Said When I Wasn't Listening," "Feedback"

Parallax: "A Wineglass Full of Nails"

Pivot: "Valentine Despite Valentine's Day"

Poemeleon: "Just Trying to Get to Sandusky, He Said," "The Look of a Bay Mare"

Poetry International: "The Dogs in Dutch Paintings"

Fiera Lingue: Poets' Corner: "Thanksgiving Snow"

Prairie Schooner: "Which Is to Say"

Salt River Review: "Letters from the Dead"

Sycamore Review: "Long Overdue Note to My College Professor. . .," "Posters the Sun Is Erasing"

Truck: "Vinegar and Fizz" (section 2, as "My Mother Goes Back to Christmas 1937")

Umbrella: "The Honey of Earth"

Verse-Virtual: "At Sixty-Five," "The Crow from Home," "Most of the Time We Live Through the Night," "Vinegar and Fizz" (section 1, as "My Mother Could Not Be Trusted"), "New Year Love," "Ode to the Faces in Renaissance Paintings,"

"The Pump Handle," "Small Round Valentine," "Tim's Tale" (as "Tim"), "Why I Love America"

Verse Wisconsin: "David Divides His Time," "Splash"

Wisconsin Academy Review: "How Would Jesus Drive?"

"Heaven Changes" was published in *In Like Company: The Salt River Review & Porch Anthology,* ed. James Cervantes (MadHat Press, 2014).

"The Dogs in Dutch Paintings" was reprinted in *180 More: Extraordinary Poems For Every Day*, ed. Billy Collins (Random House, 2005); *The Breath of Parted Lips: Voices from the Robert Frost Place:* (CavanKerry Press, 2001); *Poetry Daily: 366 Poems from the World's Most Popular Poetry Website*, eds. Diane Boller, Don Selby, & Chryss Yost (Sourcebooks, 2003); and *Seriously Funny: Poems about Love, Death, Religion, Art, Politics, Sex, and Everything Else,* eds. Barbara Hamby & David Kirby (University of Georgia Press, 2010).

"Homage to Sadie Bosheers" was reprinted in *The Breath of Parted Lips: Voices from the Robert Frost Place:* (CavanKerry Press, 2001).

"How Would Jesus Drive?" was reprinted in *Sweet Jesus: Poems About the Ultimate Icon,* eds. Nick Carbo and Denise Duhamel (Anthology Press, 2002).

"Long Overdue Note to My College Professor. . ." was reprinted in *In Praise of Pedagogy: Poetry, Flash Fiction, and Essays on Composing*, eds. Wendy Bishop & David Starkey (Calendar Island Publishers, 2000); *Letters to the World: Poems from the Wom-Po Listserv,* eds. Moira Richards, Rosemary Starace, & Lesley Wheeler (Red Hen Press, 2008); and *From Dusk to Need: 25 Years of Flume Press,* ed. Casey Huff (Flume Press, 2010).

"The Look of a Bay Mare" was reprinted in *The Best of the Net 2009*, ed. Patricia Smith (Sundress Publications, 2009).

"Splash" was reprinted in *Wisconsin Poets' Calendar 2013*, eds. Sarah Busse & Wendy Vardaman (Wisconsin Fellowship of Poets, 2012).

"Summons" was reprinted in *The Breath of Parted Lips: Voices from the Robert Frost Place.:* (CavanKerry Press, 2001).

"A Wineglass Full of Nails" was reprinted in *CrossConnect: Writers of the Information Age III*, ed. D. Edward Deifer (CrossConnect, 1999*)*.

"The Dogs in Dutch Paintings." "Homage to Sadie Bosheers," "Long Overdue Note...," "Posters the Sun Is Erasing," "Summons," and "Valentine Despite Valentine's Day," appeared in *Stutter Monk*, a limited-edition chapbook (Flume Press, 2000).

"The Dogs in Dutch Paintings" was translated into Spanish by Oscar E. Aguilera and featured in *Pares Cum Paribus* (Fall-Winter 1997).

"The Dogs in Dutch Paintings" was featured on *Poetry Daily* for April 25, 1999.

Deep thanks to friends, colleagues, and former students in Wisconsin for decades of support. A tip of the hat also to Firestone Feinberg, bright light in the poetry world. A number of poems in this book would not exist without the correspondence, inspiration, and friendship of Brent Goodman, Eric Nelson, Kate Sontag, and the late Barry Spacks. I also owe a debt of gratitude to The Frost Place and its people for crucial support. Let me raise a special toast to Sydney Lea, for his early and ongoing support. And to the late Don Sheehan, who provided a stellar example of what a healthy community of writers looks like. His influence on my writing, my teaching, and my life has been enduring.

About the Author

David Graham has published two full-length collections of poetry, *Magic Shows* and *Second Wind*, as well as four chapbooks, most recently *Stutter Monk*. He is also co-editor of *After Confession: Poetry as Autobiography* (with Kate Sontag) and *Local News: Poetry About Small Towns* (with Tom Montag). He retired in 2016 from teaching writing and literature at Ripon College, where he also hosted the Visiting Writers Series for twenty-eight years. He has served on The Poets' Prize Committee and the Wisconsin Poet Laureate Commission and was a Resident Poet and a faculty member at The Frost Place. Currently he is a contributing editor for *Verse-Virtual,* where he contributes a monthly column, "Poetic License," on poetry and poets. After retiring, he returned to his native upstate New York with his wife, the artist Lee Shippey.

www.davidgrahampoet.com

CPSIA information can be obtained
at www.ICGtesting.com
Printed in the USA
LVHW091633230719
625023LV00004B/626/P